MW01717233

The Spy Down the Street

A WOODLAND MYSTERY

By Irene Schultz

Wright Group
McGraw-Hill

To my brother Lee, and his courage that is a model for others to follow

The Spy Down the Street

Cover and cameo illustrations by Taylor Bruce
Interior illustrations by Meredith Yasui, Tom Boatman, and Charles Solway
Map illustration by Alicia Kramer

Wright Group/McGraw-Hill
19201 120th Avenue NE, Suite 100
Bothell, WA 98011
www.WrightGroup.com

Printed in the United States of America

10 9 8 7

ISBN: 0-7802-7240-4
ISBN: 0-7802-7938-7 (6-pack)

What family solves mysteries...has adventures all over the world...and loves oatmeal cookies?

It's the Woodlanders!

Sammy Westburg (10 years old)
His sister Kathy Westburg (13)
His brother Bill Westburg (14)
His best friend Dave Briggs (16)
His best grown-up friend Mrs. Tandy
And Mop, their little dog!

The children all lost their parents, but with Mrs. Tandy have made their own family.

Why are they called the Woodlanders? Because they live in a big house in the Bluff Lake woods. On Woodland Street!

Together they find fun, mystery, and adventure. What are they up to now?

Read on!

Meet the Woodlanders!

Sammy Westburg
Sammy is a ten-year-old wonder! He's big for his fifth-grade class, and big-mouthed, too. He has wild hair and makes awful spider faces. Even so, you can't help liking him.

Bill Westburg
Bill, fourteen, is friendly and strong, and only one inch taller than his brother Sammy. He loves Sammy, but pokes him to make him be quiet! He's in junior high.

Kathy Westburg
Kathy, thirteen, is small, shy, and smart. She wants to be a doctor someday! She loves to be with Dave, and her brothers kid her about it. She's in junior high, too.

Dave Briggs

Dave, sixteen, is tall and blond. He can't walk, so he uses a wheelchair and drives a special car. He likes coaching high-school sports, solving mysteries, and reading. And Kathy!

Mrs. Tandy

Sometimes the kids call her Mrs. T. She's Becky Tandy, their tall, thin, caring friend. She's always ready for a new adventure, and for making cookies!

Mop

Mop is the family's little tan dog. Sometimes they have to leave him behind with friends. But he'd much rather be running after Sammy.

Table of Contents

Chapter 1:
The Garage Sale

Fourteen-year-old Bill Westburg came running through the woods.

He rushed into his house in Bluff Lake.

He yelled at the top of his voice, "EVERYBODY! WAKE UP! COME ON!"

He raced to the other end of the house.

He ran into the big bedroom he shared with his sixteen-year-old friend, Dave Briggs.

Dave looked up and yawned.

Bill said, "Come on, Dave, there's a garage sale down the street! Let's go, before all the good stuff is gone!"

Dave pulled himself out of bed and into his wheelchair.

Ten-year-old Sammy, standing in the hall in his shorts, shouted, "Bill, this better be good!

"It's only eight thirty, and it's Saturday!

"Why did you wake me up?"

Bill yelled back, "I saw a sign on the corner, on a tree. It says there's a garage sale a couple of blocks away!"

Sammy shouted, "Well, why didn't you

say so in the first place?" He threw on his clothes.

Thirteen-year-old Kathy looked sleepy. She said, "A garage sale? I love those."

Mrs. Tandy hurried out of the kitchen. "Did somebody say garage sale? Let's go!"

The five Woodlanders got ready to go in ten minutes.

Before they left, Mrs. Tandy handed around a plate of fresh-baked muffins. They were hot, with butter melted on them.

She said, "Here, take as many as you want!"

Everyone took two or three, except for Sammy, who took four.

He put one into his mouth, and bit off half of it.

Bill said, "You look like a snapping turtle!"

Sammy said, "I bet even a snapping turtle would love these!

"Mrs. Tandy, you're the best muffin-maker in Bluff Lake.

"No ... in the United States.

"No ... in all of North America."

Mrs. Tandy said, "Is that all? I thought I was the best muffin-maker in the world!

"Now let's go to that sale."

Talking and laughing, they piled outside with Mop, their shaggy tan dog.

They found the sign that Bill had seen.

When they got there, they saw an open garage with tables all around.

The tables were covered with things for sale.

There were dishes and cups and clothes and old toys.

There were shoes and purses and boxes and bottles.

There were books and old pencils and kitchen things and baskets and magazines.

Mop ran around, sniffing everything.

Kathy said, “Look! Here’s an old chemistry set! And it still has almost all of the test tubes and chemicals!”

Dave said, “It doesn’t cost much, either. Let’s get it.”

Bill said, “Look at this pile of magazines. Camera magazines and some about travel. I’m getting these!”

Mrs. Tandy said, “Here’s a nice big

roaster. It's just the size I want. But it's missing the lid."

A thin, tired-looking woman sat at a table in front of the garage, next to the open door.

A two-year-old boy was playing at her feet.

Mrs. Tandy said, "Hello, there! I can use this roaster the way it is, but do you think you might have the top to it somewhere in the house?"

The woman nodded.

"Maybe," she whispered.

Mrs. Tandy said, "I'll leave you my phone number. If you come across the lid, would you call me?"

She wrote down her name and phone number, and gave it to her.

The woman folded the paper and put it in her pocket.

Then Sammy ran over with a blue leather box, about the size of a deck of cards.

He opened it and said, "Look, Mrs. Tandy! It's a folding clock. Just like yours! Same color and everything. Exactly!

"I love yours. I'm getting this one."

Bill said, "But it doesn't work, Sammy. I tried it."

Sammy said, "Then I'll have it fixed. I can take it to the clock shop."

Finally they had seen it all.

They paid for their things.

Sammy put the clock into his pocket.

But just as they were walking away, a shiny black car pulled up to the house.

A big, bearded man jumped out.

His eyes flashed with anger.

Mop started barking his head off.

The little boy started to cry.

The man ran toward the garage, shouting, "Selma, you fool! What do you think you're doing! Why have you let strangers come to my home!"

Chapter 2:
A Family Fight

The big man leaned over his wife's table.

His face was almost touching hers. He grabbed her arm in an iron hold.

The woman looked very scared.

She moved back as far as she could in her chair.

She looked like she wanted to get away from his awful face.

She whispered, "Kurt! You said you would be gone all weekend!"

He growled, "Well, I'm back, Selma, and this is the last time I'm EVER leaving you alone."

He turned to the other people in the garage.

He shouted, "This sale is a mistake. So get out of here! Now!"

Then he turned back to Selma. He hissed, "You're crazy. I can't trust you."

The Woodlanders stood on the sidewalk, listening to the whole thing.

Sammy whispered to Bill, "She didn't seem crazy to me, just scared. HE seems crazy."

Kathy said, "I feel so sorry for her."

Mrs. Tandy said, "I wouldn't stay with a man like that for a minute."

The man pulled his wife up from her chair. He pushed her toward the house.

Suddenly, before anyone could stop him, Sammy ran up to them.

He grabbed the man's arm.

He shouted, "Stop pushing her, you big rat!"

The man spun around like a top.

He let go of his wife and grabbed Sammy instead, by both wrists.

But Sammy was strong. He was able to yank his arms loose.

Bill ran up and shouted, "Leave my brother alone, mister. Come on, Sammy."

The man said, "You two brats better keep out of my family business."

Bill said quickly, "You'd better treat your wife better, or we will tell Police Chief Hemster about it."

The man suddenly changed. He tried to sound friendly.

He said to his wife, "Run on into the house, Selma."

She picked up her son and hurried inside.

Then he turned back to Bill. He said in a smooth voice, "I'm sorry if I was rude. I'm just so worried about poor Selma."

Sammy said, "What do you mean? What's wrong with her?"

Bill said, "Come on, Sammy. You don't want to get mixed up in this."

But Sammy said, "Yes, I do. What IS wrong with her?"

The man said, "She imagines things. She makes up wild stories. She thinks people are trying to hurt her. I shouldn't have left her alone."

Bill said, "That's too bad. Well, we have to go now."

He yanked Sammy by the arm and pulled him along.

When they joined the others, Sammy said, "I guess I was wrong to butt in. He probably isn't so bad.

"He told us about his wife's problem."

But Bill said, "No, Sammy. You were right!"

Kathy said, "Why, Bill? What makes you so sure?"

Bill said, "He says his wife is crazy.

But he also said she thinks people are trying to hurt her.

"If that were true, she would never have had a garage sale."

Mrs. Tandy said, "Why, I believe you're right, Bill. But why would he say that about her?"

Then Sammy said, "You know, I think there's something else fishy about him.

"First he called us brats. But the minute Bill said Chief Hemster's name, he started acting nice."

Dave said, "This is just too weird. Maybe we should tell the chief about him, just in case."

Mrs. Tandy said, "Well, it's ten fifteen now, and we should make a real breakfast. No, a brunch.

"Why don't we call John Hemster and ask him to eat with us?

"Then we can tell him about all this."

Sammy said, "Sure, that's a great idea. Then you can see your BOYFRIEND again!"

Mrs. Tandy grabbed Sammy and hugged him.

She said, "You know YOU'RE my boyfriend, Sammy. You have eyes that could melt the heart of a truck!"

Sammy turned bright red.

When they got home, Mrs. Tandy said, "Well, I'll make a couple of pans of corn bread. Sammy, you can help me."

Dave said, "I'll make my famous hot dogs and eggs if you want."

Kathy said, "Great! I'll call Chief Hemster, then Bill and I can set the table."

When Chief Hemster got there, Mop gave him his usual tail-wagging, finger-licking greeting.

Then they all sat down to eat brunch.

Dave said, "Chief Hemster, we saw something this morning we want to tell you about. We went to a garage sale that got called off."

Chief Hemster laughed.

He said, "Well, that's not exactly going to make the evening news. Something else must have happened!"

Sammy said, "It did! There was a nice woman running it, and she almost got beaten up by her husband Kurt.

"Her name was Selma.

"See, he didn't know she was having the sale. He was out of town.

"But he came home early and—"

Just then the phone rang.

Mrs. Tandy picked it up.

A woman's voice said, "I need help. Can I come to talk—"

Then the phone clicked dead.

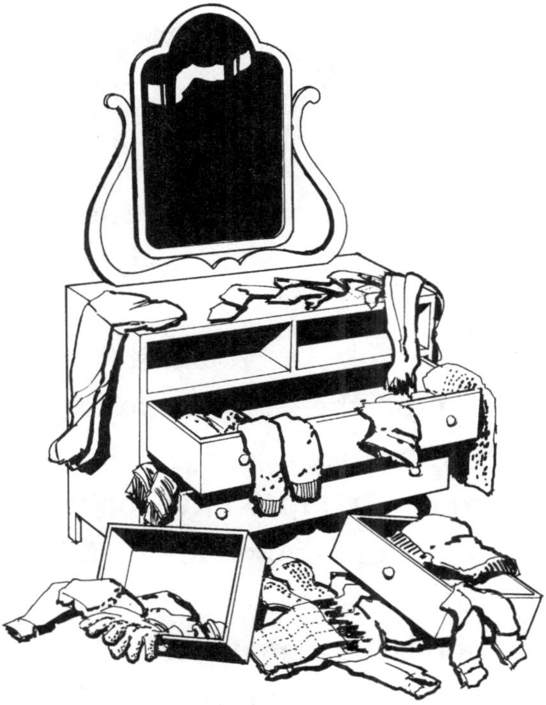

Chapter 3: The Break-In

Mrs. Tandy looked shaken.

She sat down at the table.

She said, "That was a woman calling for help. She sounded scared."

Bill said, "Who was it?"

Mrs. Tandy said, "I'm not sure. But I think it sounded like Selma.

"All she said was, 'I need help.' Then she said, 'Can I come to talk,' and the line went dead."

Kathy said, "Oh, no! Do you think it WAS that woman at the sale? Maybe her husband's hurting her again."

Mrs. Tandy said, "It must have been her. But how would she know our phone number?"

Dave said, "Don't you remember? You gave her your number so she could call you if she found the roaster lid."

Chief Hemster said, "It makes sense. Maybe she watched you at the garage sale. Maybe she saw how friendly you are.

"Maybe she has no friends of her own to turn to.

"Tell me everything that happened."

So they told him about buying their things, and Kurt coming home, and Sammy and Bill standing up to him.

Chief Hemster said, "She must be the one who called.

"It's clear she's in some sort of trouble. She probably heard someone coming and hung up. I bet she will call again.

"I'll keep an eye on her house. And I'll see what I can find out about the family."

Bill said, "We can help. We Woodlanders have our ways!"

Chief Hemster said, "Don't I know it. Talk to you later!" He left to talk to his officers.

Sammy said, "Before I forget, I'm going to ride my bike up to Green Forest and take my clock in to be fixed."

Dave said, "Let's clean up here. Then

we can all drive into Green Forest together.

"You can drop off your clock.

"Then we can do the grocery shopping. And then find out what we can about Selma and Kurt."

They piled into Dave's station wagon. It had hand controls, so he could drive it easily.

When they came home, they found the front door un-locked.

As they walked inside, Bill said, "Uh-oh! We are in BIG trouble!"

Everything in the living room and kitchen was a mess. All the cabinets and drawers were open.

Someone had searched the house!

They put their grocery bags on the kitchen table. Then they looked around in the dining room.

Every drawer in the room had been dumped out onto the table.

Every cabinet had been emptied onto the floor.

Some dishes had been broken.

Kathy heard a scratching sound coming from the front closet. She said, "MOP! It's Mop!"

She ran to open the door.

There stood poor little Mop, in a pile

of rubber boots, almost covered by coats.

He had some blood on one side of his mouth.

Kathy hugged him and said, "Oh, you poor baby. Someone kicked you into this closet.

"I'll get you washed off, and see if we have to take you to the vet."

The others kept looking around.

Some of the other rooms were just as bad.

All the clothes in Sammy's and Kathy's drawers had been dumped out.

All the bathroom cupboards were emptied onto the floor.

But when they got to Mrs. Tandy's room, they found something very strange.

Only the first two drawers of her dresser had been dumped. The third drawer was standing open. And the bottom one hadn't been touched.

Dave said, "Looks like we scared them before they could finish."

Then he checked the windows in the room.

He said, "That's funny. They didn't get out through these windows."

They checked the rest of the house. Every window and door was locked from the inside, except the front door.

Dave said, "The only way they could have left is through this door.

"And we would've seen them if they ran out right when we came home.

"That means we didn't scare them away. They found whatever they wanted and left before we got home."

Bill said, "Then let's go back to Mrs. T.'s room. They must've found what they wanted in that third drawer."

They all hurried back to her room.

Mop went with them, dancing and barking.

Mrs. Tandy looked into the drawer. It was one big mess.

She said, "I keep my scarves and gloves in here, and my socks.

"I keep purses and belts in it, too. I can't imagine what they could have wanted out of here."

She began putting her things into neat piles.

She said, "Here are all my scarves, I think. And my purses and belts. Nope, I think it's all here."

Kathy said, "Do you think the people who broke in were just messing around? Just some stupid people who like to break things?"

Dave said, "It sure looks like it."

Bill said, "Well, let's call Chief Hemster and—HEY! Everybody! Move back from the window!"

Chapter 4: Followed!

Sammy said, "What's wrong, Bill?"

Bill said, "I saw a man sneaking through the woods! He was looking toward the house. Right at us!"

Dave said, "What did he look like? Was it anyone you know?"

Bill said, "No. In fact, I bet he's not even from Bluff Lake."

Mrs. Tandy was still standing at her dresser. She said, "What makes you say that?"

Bill said, "He was wearing a business suit. Hardly anyone in Bluff Lake wears suits, even during the week. And this is Saturday."

Mrs. Tandy pretended to look into her drawer. But she looked to the side, out the window.

Without moving her head she began to talk. "I can see him right now.

"He's just standing there watching me.

"He's behind a honeysuckle bush, but I can still see him."

Kathy looked scared. She whispered, "Shouldn't we call the police?"

Then Mrs. Tandy said, "My lands! There's another person out there, too. And do you know who it is? The garage-sale man! Kurt!"

Bill said, "OK, guys, we have to call Chief Hemster. It looks like those two must be the ones who searched the house."

Dave said, "Right. And maybe they didn't find what they wanted after all. Why else would they still be hanging around?"

Chief Hemster was there in five minutes.

He took one look around at the mess.

He said, "First of all, next time you find your house in this shape, DON'T GO IN!

"LEAVE RIGHT AWAY, and call the police! You were just lucky those guys weren't still in your house!

"Here's what we have to do. I'll look for fingerprints later. But for now, let's see if we can catch them breaking in again.

"Let's get out of here. Then one of my officers and I will circle around and hide in the woods. We can keep watch on those two.

"The rest of you go see what you can find out about Kurt and Selma."

So they all left the house.

Mrs. Tandy and Kathy went to talk to

some friends who lived near Kurt and Selma's house.

Dave went to talk to his friend Tom, who did the trash pick-up. He always seemed to know everything that was going on.

But Bill and Sammy had another plan.

They crossed the street and walked half a block. Then they slipped behind a bush. They were going to turn around and sneak back to watch their house.

They looked back.

Sammy whispered, "Holy cats! Those two guys are coming out of our woods! They're not going back into our house!"

Bill said, "Hey! I thought WE were following THEM! But it looks like they are following US!"

Sammy said, "Let's find out! Let's lead them on a wild goose chase!"

Dragging Bill, he stepped back onto

the sidewalk. The two boys walked quickly toward the next corner.

They turned the corner, and took a look back.

The men were halfway up the block, still coming after them.

Bill said, "Come on, Sammy. Follow me!"

The boys began to jog along, around the next corner to the right.

They saw Kurt and the other man coming after them.

Sammy said, "What do we do now?"

Bill said, "Might as well tire them out a little."

He looked to make sure no cars were coming.

Then he darted across the street with Sammy.

Sammy saw where Bill was taking him.

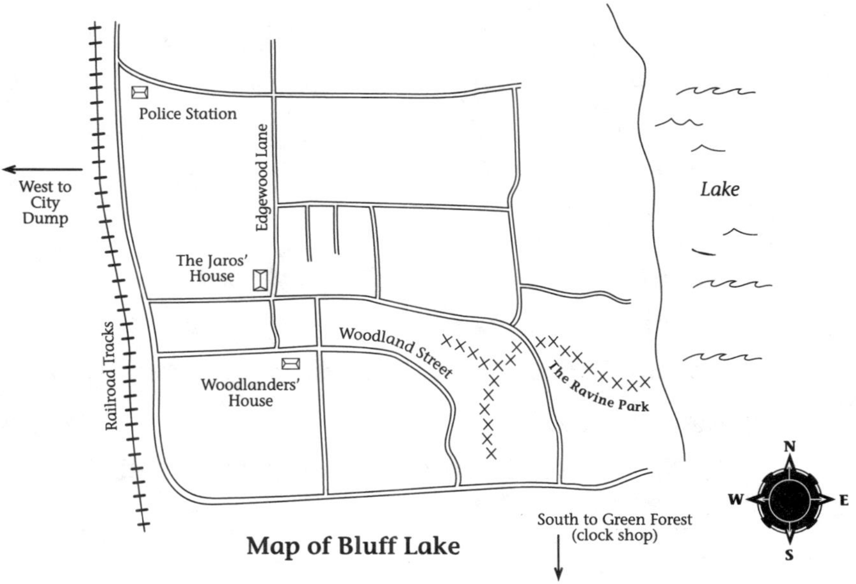

Map of Bluff Lake

He said, "Perfect! The Ravine Park!"

The Ravine Park of Bluff Lake wasn't like some parks.

It wasn't flat.

It didn't have swings.

It didn't have a baseball field.

It was just a deep ravine—a canyon full of bushes and trees.

It went on for half a mile, right to the lake. A stream ran through it.

Sammy and Bill ran along the ravine path. It wound through the bushes, above the stream.

They ran until the bushes hid them. Then they turned around to look back.

Along came the two men, groaning and talking.

Sammy whispered, "Those rats are still behind us!"

The men pushed their way along the path.

Branches slapped their faces.

They tripped on tree roots and bumps.

The man in the suit kept sliding off the path.

The boys heard them talking.

Kurt said, "Don't make so much noise, Antel. The boys will hear you."

Antel said, "You are the one making

the noise, Kurt.

"And you are the one who got us into this. You lost the thing, not me.

"And my boss is going to be MAD."

Kurt said, "Oh, shut up, Antel. I'm not the one who'll be in trouble with your boss if we don't get it back. You are. I'm just out some money."

Sammy whispered, "What do you think they lost? And why are they following US?"

Bill said, "Beats me. Let's move along. Make a little noise when you start so they can tell where we are.

"That way we can keep them following us. Maybe then we can find out what they're up to."

Chapter 5:
The Ravine Chase

The boys started up the path again.

They stepped on dried leaves to make noise as they walked.

The path switched to the other side of

the stream. They crossed over the stream on a fallen tree trunk.

Antel kept slipping, muttering angry words in a language that wasn't English.

The men began to huff and puff from the heat.

Soon the boys were far ahead. They stepped off the path behind some bushes and circled back, above the men.

Bill and Sammy stood as still as trees and watched them.

Antel had sweat running down his face.

He stopped to take off his coat. Kurt's face was shining red.

Sammy whispered, "Look at him, with his red face and that black beard. He looks like a monster."

Bill whispered, "His friend with the suit SOUNDS like a monster, he's so mad."

The men came to the tree-trunk bridge, over the stream.

Antel started across.

Suddenly the boys heard him shout. He almost fell.

He let go of his coat.

It landed in the water and mud below.

Antel growled.

Kurt stood and laughed at him. He said, "I told you not to wear that stupid suit and those shiny black shoes here in Bluff Lake!"

Antel was mad! He said, "Go down and get my coat, NOW!"

Kurt said, "Get it yourself."

Antel finally fished his coat out of the stream.

He got his shoes all muddy.

He hissed, "I don't know why we are even here. Those kids probably don't have it with them.

"And even if they do, how will we get them to give it to us?"

Kurt said, "I can get them to give it to me. Don't worry about that.

"Let's get going. I'm tired of your whining."

Sammy poked Bill. He said, "Holy smoke! They think we have something of theirs!

"Why would they think that? We better get away from here!"

The boys hurried ahead through the ravine.

Bill said, "The longer we can lead them on, the more we can find out."

Sammy and Bill kept making noise ... so the men could follow them.

The boys laughed out loud.

Or they talked loudly.

They stomped on some twigs.

Or they kicked some stones into the stream.

The next time Sammy and Bill sneaked back to listen, they heard Antel say, "Stop for a second, Kurt. I have a stone in my shoe."

Kurt said, "Hurry up! We've almost got those kids in our hands!

"Do you think the brats know what they have? Why did they take it if they aren't on to us?"

Antel said, "Maybe it was just chance.

Still, they may know.

"They all seem to be very close with the police."

Kurt said, "In this country, the police are often friends of children. That doesn't mean they're working together!

"Come on! You have your shoe on again.

"Let's not lose them."

Bill and Sammy went running ahead.

Bill said, "Sammy, I don't know what this is all about, but I'm not sure how smart we are, doing this. Those guys sound mean."

Sammy said, "Don't worry, Bill. I'll take care of us."

They came to a huge metal pipe, so big they could almost stand up in it.

It ran under a road that crossed the ravine. The stream ran right through the pipe, about six inches deep.

The boys rolled up their pants and waded through the water.

Then they climbed to some high bushes and looked down. They waited for the men to come through the pipe.

Antel was as mad as a BULL!

Now he had his shoes and socks in one hand.

His nice pants were rolled up and all wrinkled.

He had his wet, muddy coat in the other hand.

He said, "My feet are cut to pieces. My clothes are ruined. And it's all your fault, Kurt! You lost that thing to some kids! I'll get you for this!"

Kurt said, "Don't worry. When I get my hands on them, I'll—"

Just then a rock under Sammy's hand came loose. He began to slip. He fell right through the bushes.

He grabbed at a bush.

Bill tried to stop Sammy's fall. But Sammy went sliding all the way down the side of the ravine.

He landed right at the feet of Kurt and Antel.

Kurt grabbed Sammy by the arm. He tried to lift him to his feet. But Sammy just sat there on the ground, not moving one inch.

Kurt growled, "This kid is a bag of cement! Get up, kid. Where's the other boy?"

Sammy said, "I don't want to get up. My foot hurts. Leave me alone."

Then Bill came sliding down the ravine wall. He came to a stop in front of Kurt, too.

He was holding a heavy tree branch, bigger than a baseball bat.

He lifted it above his head.

He said, "Get your hands off my brother!"

Kurt let go of Sammy's arm. He took a step back.

Just then they all heard a sound from the top of the ravine.

A man's voice called, "You having some trouble down there?"

They looked up.

There stood Chief Hemster!

And Officer Sanchez!

Chapter 6: Up to No Good

Chief Hemster came half-walking, half-sliding, down the wall of the ravine.

He looked from Antel to Kurt.

Then he looked at Bill, standing there

with his branch, and Sammy, holding his sore foot.

He said, "You boys need some help?"

Kurt spoke up before the boys could answer.

He said, "No, we can handle it. I was showing my friend the wonderful Ravine Park.

"We found this boy on the ground. I was just trying to help him up."

Sammy opened his mouth in surprise.

He said, "Hey, wait a minute—"

But Bill stopped him. He looked straight at him and winked.

Sammy kept quiet.

Bill said, "Glad to see you, Chief.

"Now that you're here, maybe you can help me get Sammy up to the top, and home. He hurt his foot.

"He can use this branch as a walking stick."

Chief Hemster said, "Sure, Bill. Let's go right up the side. You choose the way."

He turned to the men. He said, "Good-bye, gentlemen. Thanks for being so helpful."

Then he and Bill helped Sammy up the ravine to the street at the top.

Sammy said, "Boy, was I glad to see you, Chief! And you, too, Officer Sanchez!

"How did you know where to find us? And how did you know we were in trouble?"

Chief Hemster said, "We've been following you ever since the men left the woods behind your house.

"They weren't waiting to go into the house. They'd been waiting to go after you!"

Officer Sanchez said, "The six of us

following each other must have looked like a parade!"

Sammy said, "No telling what would have happened if you hadn't followed us."

Chief Hemster said, "It looked to me like Bill had it all under control without us."

Sammy hit Bill on the arm.

He said, "Why did you want me to be quiet, anyway? Didn't you want Chief Hemster to know what we heard those guys saying?"

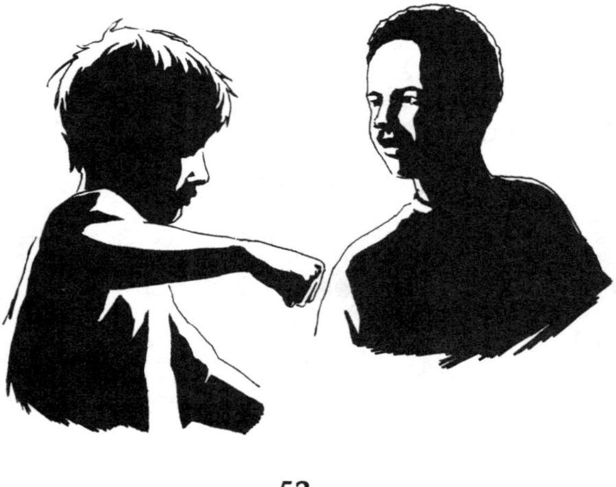

Bill said, "Sure, Sammy. I just didn't want those creeps to know we had heard it. But first, how's your foot?"

Sammy said, "OK, I guess. I just twisted it.

"I can use your stick to walk."

So they started back to the house. On the way the boys told Chief Hemster and Officer Sanchez about what they heard the men say.

While all this was going on, Dave had driven to the city dump.

He saw his friend Tom near the pond, feeding bread to the ducks.

Dave watched them paddle across the pond.

Then Tom waved and walked over to Dave's car. He said, "Hi! What's up, Dave?"

Dave said, "Hey, I need to ask you

something. Do you know a man named Kurt? He lives a couple of blocks away from us."

Tom said, "Sure. You must mean Kurt Jaro. Keeps to himself, mostly.

"Used to be in the navy.

"Mean as a rattlesnake, that guy.

"Big bully.

"Beady blue eyes. Beard.

"Orders his wife around.

"I know they have a kid, too, about two years old. Paul, I think."

Dave laughed. He said, "You sure know a lot about him. How did you find all that out?"

Tom said, "Oh, you can learn a lot about people by picking up their garbage.

"I go to that house twice a week! They moved in about three years ago. That's a lot of visits.

"I've heard him boss his wife around.

"I've heard him yell at the baby.

"I even saw him slap his kid once, hard. I called to him through the window of my truck.

"When he realized I had seen him, he turned nice as pie.

"Said he just lost his temper, and it wouldn't happen again.

"The kid's skinny like his mother, but cute as a button.

"Now Kurt shouts at them to come inside every time I come by."

Dave asked, "Do you know what he does for a living?"

Tom said, "I have no idea. He drives a nice new black car. I do know he's gone a lot. Sometimes for a week or more.

"His wife told me that one day. But when I asked her what kind of work he did, she didn't say."

Dave said, "He doesn't sound like much of a husband or father to me. But here's the weirdest part. We caught him spying on our house earlier today."

Tom said, "Really? That IS weird. And funny you should use the word 'spying.'"

Dave asked, "Why?"

Tom said, "Because one day I was at their house getting the garbage.

"Some papers from one of the cans flew out. They landed below an open window.

"So I walked over to pick them up.

"Suddenly a man leaned out the window. He called inside, 'Kurt! Someone is spying on us! Get over here!'

"Kurt came to the window. He leaned out and gave me a fake smile.

"Said he was sorry for his friend's bad manners. But I noticed he closed the window.

"I wondered what made them so nervous. Maybe I was imagining things, but I thought the two of them might be up to no good.

"I thought maybe THEY were the ones who were spying on ME."

Chapter 7:
A Terrible Chance

Mrs. Tandy and Kathy walked past Kurt and Selma's house.

They stopped at the next-door neighbors' house.

A woman came to the door.

Kathy said, "Excuse me, but do you know anything about the people next door ... on that side?"

She said, "Well, I'm afraid I can't help you much. Selma hardly ever leaves her yard. She's always pleasant to talk to, but very shy.

"Kurt Jaro never speaks to me, except when I'm working at the bookstore in town.

"He bought a few books on cameras, and guns. And once he bought a book on codes, I think."

Mrs. Tandy gave Kathy a quick look. She said, "Well, thanks for your help!" and they started for home.

Kathy said, "I sure hope the others found out more than we did."

Mrs. Tandy said, "But, Kathy, we found out a lot! Cameras? Guns? Codes?

Those are all things that SPIES use!"

They hurried back to the house.

Bill and Sammy told them about the ravine chase.

Dave told them what Tom had said.

Then Mrs. Tandy told them what the bookstore clerk had said.

Sammy said, "CODES! Like SPY codes?"

Dave said, "You know, that's the third time I've heard the word SPY today.

"And it's always when people are talking about Kurt Jaro. He's up to something."

Chief Hemster said, "You're right, Dave. I believe those men are into something very serious. But we have no real proof yet.

"And they probably were the ones who searched the house. But we can't prove that, either.

"In our country, a person's innocent

until proven guilty, you know."

Sammy said, "But Chief Hemster, Kurt and Antel thought we had something of theirs. And they followed us.

"They're at least guilty of that.

"And I think they would have hurt us if I hadn't scared them off."

Bill said, "YOU scared them off! They were scared because Chief Hemster and I ran down to save you!"

Sammy said, "Well, you guys DID help some, I guess. But what I mean is, they are two bad men!"

Just then there was a little knock on the door.

Mrs. Tandy got up. She said, "I'll get it. And then we can get some food ready. My goodness, no one has eaten since brunch!"

She opened the front door.

There stood Selma Jaro!

Mrs. Jaro gasped, "Please. Please, I must talk to you. I only have a minute."

Mrs. Tandy led her to the living room, where the others were sitting.

She said, "Please sit down."

Mrs. Jaro said, "I have taken a terrible chance. I left my son with a neighbor for ten minutes and sneaked away.

"My husband is out driving his friend somewhere.

"I must run away from my husband, and I have no place to go. I need to take my baby from that house before it's too late.

"When Kurt came home today he was very angry. You saw him shout at me. After you left he pushed us around."

Mrs. Jaro twisted her thin hands and looked down at her lap.

She said, "I thought you might know where I could go to be safe. If you know of a place, I want to go there tonight."

Bill said, "Chief, do you know of any women's shelters in Bluff Lake?"

Chief Hemster said, "No. But if you need help, you can always come to the police station.

"We can also find a safe house in the

city if we have to."

Bill said, "Why couldn't she stay here, Mrs. T.? We have the guest room in the basement."

Mrs. Tandy said, "That's a fine idea, Bill."

Mrs. Jaro said, "Oh, no! I couldn't do that."

Mrs. Tandy said, "Nonsense! Stay with us. You'll be safe here."

Mrs. Jaro was crying now.

She said, "But I can't tell you why my husband acts as he does. And how can you help me unless I tell you everything?"

Dave wheeled over to her. He said, "Mrs. Tandy and Bill and Sammy and Kathy helped me when I was in trouble. Now we all want to help you.

"Go home and come back with your little boy as soon as you can."

Chief Hemster said, "Dave's right. Head on home to get your things. And if you have trouble getting away, turn on an upstairs light.

"Then pull a shade up and down. I'll be watching your house after dark. I'll come to your door and get you if you can't get away before then."

Mrs. Jaro got up.

She went to the door.

She said, "I have to go now. I can never thank you enough.

"Thank you. I'll try to come back tonight."

She slipped out the door.

Chapter 8: The Stinker

Sammy said, "This is going to be perfect! At last! Someone younger than me living in this house!

"I can be an older brother, like Bill,

and boss him around.

"I'll get their bedroom ready with you, Mrs. Tandy."

Chief Hemster said, "Well, I'll get to the station. Keep me posted!"

The Woodlanders started getting ready for their visitors.

Mrs. Tandy and Sammy made the bed in the basement. Then they emptied two drawers for Selma and Paul to use.

Sammy picked some wildflowers from the woods and put them in a vase on the desk.

He said, "There, maybe these will make Mrs. Jaro feel better."

Bill came down and said, "Hey, this looks good! Come on up, Sammy. We are doing our homework.

"It looks like we might be pretty busy the rest of the weekend, once Mrs. Jaro gets here."

Sammy said, "Aw, I want to do mine later. Maybe Sunday night."

Bill said, "Oh, OK. But Dave and Kathy said when we are done with our homework we can get out the new chemistry set."

Sammy raced up to his room and opened his books.

First he did his spelling and math.

Then he worked on his science project.

He was building two different kinds of birds' nests. He went outside to get some sticks and grass.

It was only 5:00, but it was getting dark. The front woods were full of shadows.

Still, Sammy found what he needed.

He was just turning around to go inside when he saw something.

Sticking out from under a bunch of tall bushes was a man's shoe.

He couldn't see the rest of the man, just one foot.

Sammy made himself stay calm.

Quietly, he walked into the house and closed the door.

He called, "Bill! Dave! Kathy! Quick! I have to tell you something! Mrs. Tandy! Come here!

"I saw Kurt's shoe out there! I know it was his because Antel's shoes are black! That creep is hiding in our woods again!"

Kathy said, "Oh, no! What if he sees Mrs. Jaro and Paul on their way here! What if he grabs her the minute she walks up our driveway?"

Mrs. Tandy said, "That rotten stinker! First he hurts Selma. Now he may stop her from getting help!"

Bill said, "STINKER?

"Mrs. Tandy, did you say STINKER?

"Now I know how we can get Kurt

out of the woods!

"First, one of us has to stay hidden near the Jaros' house ... and watch for Mrs. Jaro and Paul.

"When they come out, that person can bring them here through all the back-yards.

"They can go through the holes in the fences and between the houses, and around the tall bushes, until they're across the street from our driveway."

Sammy said, "The neighbors are always telling me to stop taking those short-cuts.

"Now I can cut through their yards and be a hero instead of a pest! I'll be the one to get Mrs. Jaro!

"And I can help her carry Paul, too."

Dave said, "But what's the rest of the plan? What's the STINKER part?"

Bill said, "Easy, Dave. You and Kathy are chemistry whizzes.

"You guys figure out what to use from the chemistry set to make a stink bomb!

"Remember when Mrs. Cheng made that tiny one in my science class the last day of school ... and I came home smelling bad?"

Sammy said, "BAD! A skunk would have smelled like a rose next to you!"

Kathy said, "Oh, I know how she made that."

Dave said, "Me, too. And I think I follow your stink-bomb idea, Bill. And here's how we could pull it off!

"You and Kathy and I can take the chemistry set out and pretend to be using it on the front steps.

"We can wait until Sammy gives us some signal ... maybe a birdcall ... to tell us he and Mrs. Jaro and Paul are in the bushes across from the driveway."

Sammy said, "How about a cardinal's whistle, loud, three times in a row!"

Dave said, "Perfect. You do that, then I'll start yelling, and pretend our experiment went bad.

"I'll shout at you two to throw the test tube into the woods."

Kathy said, "Yes! Then I'll drop in the stuff that makes that awful smell.

"And Bill can throw the test tube right where Kurt is hiding!"

Bill said, "If that doesn't get rid of him, he doesn't have a nose!"

Sammy said, "What a rip-off! I'll be the only one who doesn't get to make a stink bomb!"

Bill said, "Don't worry. You'll learn how from Mrs. Cheng when you get to junior high."

Dave said, "Scoot over to watch for Mrs. Jaro now, Sammy."

Mrs. Tandy said, "I'm going to get together the best dinner you ever saw.

"We are going to make Selma glad she came!

"I'll call Chief Hemster to come, too. I know he will want to talk to her."

Chapter 9: Bird Boy

Kathy, Dave, and Bill went outside.

They set up their chemistry set on the front porch steps, and began mixing chemicals.

They kept talking loudly to each other so Kurt would hear them.

Mrs. Tandy watched them from the front window.

She watched Sammy walk out of the house.

He got to the woods across from their own house, walked into them, and disappeared.

He cut through back yards to the ravine. Then he crossed the street ... to get near the Jaros' house ... to watch for Mrs. Jaro and the baby.

Kathy, Dave, and Bill kept working with the chemicals outside in the dim light.

They pretended to read the chemistry booklet to decide what to make.

They argued about what to mix next.

They kept walking over to the edge of the woods to dump their old chemical mixes.

The whole time, they were secretly keeping an eye on where Kurt was standing.

He was still right in the middle of a bunch of high bushes, all hidden except for one shoe.

And they listened for Sammy.

Kathy thought she heard a cardinal and her heart skipped a beat.

But it wasn't Sammy whistling. This bird whistled its song only one time.

Then another cardinal sang. But it sounded very far away.

Now it was dark, except for the porch light.

At last came three clear cardinal songs, one after another.

Dave winked at Kathy and Bill.

Then he yelled, "Hey, something's wrong with this mix! Get rid of it! Quick!"

Bill and Kathy ran toward the woods.

Then Bill threw the test tube right into the middle of the bush where Kurt was standing.

A horrible rotten-egg smell filled the air.

A gasping sound came out of the bush.

Then footsteps crashed away through the woods, and down the street.

Sammy darted up the front steps and into the front door, with Mrs. Jaro and Paul.

Mrs. Jaro was so tired she simply sat on the living-room couch and cried.

Mrs. Tandy said, "Why, you poor dear, let me sit next to you."

She put her arm around Mrs. Jaro and said, "I made some oatmeal cookies.

"I know it's right before dinner, but sometimes a cookie can make a person feel a lot more cheery."

Sammy said, "Good. Glad you feel that way about it, Mrs. T.!" And he took a big bunch for himself.

Mrs. Tandy said, "Go ahead, Sammy. After what you did tonight, you deserve them, you good old cardinal."

Then Mrs. Jaro smiled a little.

She said, "He is a hero. I want to thank you for coming to get us, Sammy. And please, all of you, call me Selma."

Bill said, "Sammy, from now on I'm going to call you Bird Boy."

Sammy said, "Then I might call you Stink Bomb. Hey, our plan really worked!"

Selma wiped a tear from her eye.

She said, "This is wonderful to be here, but I'm afraid. What will Kurt do when he gets home and finds us gone?"

Mrs. Tandy said, "He won't ever get to you again. Oh, my, I see some red marks on your arms."

She pulled up little Paul's shirt, and looked at his thin little body.

She said, "He has marks on him, too. Did Kurt do this?"

Selma nodded.

Mrs. Tandy's mouth became a straight line.

Her eyebrows pulled together.

Her eyes glowed with anger.

She said, "I'm going to take a quick picture of these marks right now.

"Then we will write down what Kurt has done to you and Paul.

"Maybe that will help prove to the police what kind of man he is.

"And then ... if he ever tries to come near you again ... you have a better chance of putting him in jail."

After Mrs. Tandy took the pictures, Dave and Bill set the table.

Kathy and Sammy played with Paul.

Sammy had pulled out every toy car and truck he ever owned.

Kathy had cut windows and doors in an upside-down cardboard box.

The box became a garage.

Paul was making motor noises, and driving the cars into the garage.

They heard a knock on the door. It was Chief Hemster!

He said, "I watched all the goings-on from up the street. I followed Kurt back to his house. Officer Sanchez is keeping track of him now."

Mrs. Tandy said, "John, before we sit down to dinner, I'm giving you these photos. And here's Selma's story.

"The police need to know what Selma's husband has been doing to her and Paul."

Then all eight of them sat down around the table.

Selma bowed her head and said, "I give thanks for the friends who are keeping Paul and me safe. And after dinner I have something to tell you."

Chapter 10: The Magazine Search

When dinner was over, everyone sat down in the living room.

Selma said, "I have been keeping secrets to protect someone I love very much.

"But I want to protect you, too. You

may be in danger. And you are my only friends."

Bill said, "Maybe you could at least tell us why Kurt and Antel have been following Sammy and me.

"They think we have something of theirs, but we don't think we do."

Selma said, "That is because of what I did. That is what I wanted to tell you."

Kathy said, "What do you mean?"

Selma said, "I had the garage sale. I sold things there. I wanted to make some money to run away.

"But I must have sold something of Kurt's that was important."

Sammy said, "Wow! You mean we DO have something of theirs!"

Selma said, "Yes. I know that much from what I have heard.

"If you'll only return to Kurt what you bought, I think you'll be safe. Please do it. I feel terrible that I have put you in danger."

She stopped talking. She looked all worn-out.

Mrs. Tandy said, "You could use a good night's sleep, Selma.

"Let me get you and little Paul into bed. Then the rest of us will think over what you've said."

When Mrs. Tandy returned, she said, "What in the world could it be that Kurt wants?"

Dave said, "Maybe it wasn't something in your drawer at all, Mrs. Tandy.

"Maybe they just got scared we might come home, and stopped looking before they found it."

Kathy said, "Let's see. What did we buy? The roaster ... the chemistry set ... Sammy's broken clock ... Bill's pile of magazines ..."

Sammy said, "Hey! I bet that's it! With all the talk about codes, I bet Kurt had some secret message to give to Antel.

"And he kept it in those magazines!"

Kathy said, "I bet you're right, Sammy! Where are those magazines, Bill?"

Bill said, "Under my bed. I'll go get them."

He brought in the pile.

Sammy said, "Before we start, what are we looking for, Dave? You and Chief Hemster are the ones who know the most about codes."

Dave said, "The first thing we do is look through each magazine, page by page, for any loose slips of paper."

Bill said, "Then what?"

Dave answered, "Then we can go through them to see if any of the letters have pencil or pen marks near them.

"Even tiny dots. Even pin holes."

Kathy said, "So he may have spelled out words by marking a bunch of single letters!"

Chief Hemster said, "That makes sense."

But after an hour of looking, Sammy stood up. He said, "I looked for paper slips until my brain slipped!"

Bill said, "Your brain slipped before we started. Now get back to work."

Mrs. Tandy said, "Stick with it, Sammy. We've only gone through one third of the pile."

So they worked along for another half an hour. They all started rubbing their tired eyes.

Suddenly Dave called out, "Wait a minute! I just thought of something."

Kathy asked, "What? What is it?"

Dave said, "We must be looking at the wrong garage-sale thing!

"It just hit me. If I had something I wanted to hide and save, I wouldn't EVER put it inside of magazines.

"Magazines could be thrown out too easily, anytime, by anyone."

Bill said, "Then where WOULD you hide a secret message?"

Dave said, "What about in a folding clock? In Sammy's clock!"

Suddenly Mrs. Tandy jumped up from her chair and shouted, "NOW I know what those thieves took from my drawer!"

Chapter 11: Submarine Secrets

She rushed back to her room.

The others all followed her down the hall.

She ran to her dresser.

She pulled the third drawer open.

She looked under everything.

Then she stood up and announced, "No, it's not here."

Chief Hemster said, "What, Becky?"

She said, "My folding travel clock, like Sammy's. I just remembered. I had it in this drawer. And it's not here anymore."

Sammy said, "But why would they take YOURS?"

Bill said, "Don't you get it? They didn't know she had one, too. They thought they were taking YOURS!"

Sammy said, "Then THAT'S why they were following us!

"They didn't find what they were looking for inside Mrs. Tandy's clock. So they thought we took it out.

"They didn't know they had the wrong clock!"

Kathy said, "Then whatever they were looking for isn't even in the house! It's been at the clock shop in Green Forest ever since this morning."

Sammy said, "And we poked through all those magazines for nothing! Rotten rats!"

They went back to the dining room.

Dave said, "So what's the plan?"

But just then there was a knock at the door.

Everyone jumped.

Chief Hemster walked over to the door.

He opened it slowly, and saw it was Officer Sanchez.

She had brought a report.

Chief Hemster read it carefully. It was two pages long and had a photo attached.

Then he read it again.

At last he said, "Well, Woodlanders. It looks like you really did it this time."

Dave asked, "Why? What does it say?"

Sammy chimed in, "What did we do?"

Officer Sanchez answered, "You've opened up a real hornet's nest.

"This is a report from navy detectives.

"They have had a former navy man, Kurt Jaro, under watch for a year.

"When we fed his name into the police computer, it came up with this information."

Chief Hemster laid down a photo of two men for the others to see.

Kurt Jaro and a young sailor were together in the picture.

Chief Hemster said, "The other guy is Kurt Jaro's younger brother Dan.

"He works on an atomic submarine. A year ago there was a surprise search of the sub.

"A photo of a secret sub plan turned up. It was hidden in the bunk next to Kurt's brother's.

"So the man in that bunk was put into the navy jail, and may go on trial as a spy."

Officer Sanchez went on. "But the navy has reason to believe that he may not be the guilty one. They think the real spy might be Kurt's brother Dan.

"They think he may have hidden the photo in the next bunk when the search began ... so he wouldn't get caught with it."

Kathy asked, "So why do they think it was Kurt's brother who did it?"

Officer Sanchez said, "Because the photo could only have been taken by a special camera ... and by an expert.

"The young man who is under arrest seems to know nothing about photography.

"And he had never been seen with a special camera.

"But Kurt's brother had once been seen with a small, costly camera. Another shipmate reported that, in secret.

"And he's been seen going in and out of parts of the ship he didn't belong in.

"Anyway, the navy thinks Kurt may be in on this, too. With his pal Antel."

Bill said, "Well, what do we do now? We still don't have any real proof against them."

Chief Hemster rubbed his chin with his hand.

Then he said, "If only we could catch Antel and Kurt in the act! If only we could get them with a navy secret in their hands."

Sammy said, "Right! Then POW! They would be slapped into jail. And I bet Kurt's brother could be, too!

"And the poor sailor in jail who probably was framed could go free."

Bill said, "Too bad we can't."

Dave said, "Well, why can't we? I think I know a way."

Chapter 12: Setting the Trap

Dave said, "We have a perfect set-up for trapping them."

Bill said, "What do you mean?"

Dave said, "Well, Kurt and Antel want

the clock, right? When will your clock be ready, Sammy?"

Sammy said, "The repair man said he would get to it next week. Why?"

Dave said, "That means he probably hasn't even opened it up yet."

Kathy said, "So whatever's hidden inside is still there!"

Dave said, "And if Kurt and Antel knew where that clock was, they'd go after it in a second."

Chief Hemster said, "And if what they want is in that clock, we could catch them with it! Red-handed!"

Sammy said, "So all we have to do is let them know where the clock is.

"Then we hide out there, and nab them! EASY! But ... how do we do it?"

Mrs. Tandy said, "Well, that shouldn't be too hard. I bet those fellows are outside in the woods this very minute.

"They're DYING to find out what we are talking about.

"I bet if I just strolled up to the window, and opened it, we would have some listeners.

"Should I?"

Chief Hemster said, "Just a minute, Becky. I have a few phone calls to make first."

He called the Green Forest clock shop to arrange to get a key.

Then he called another police officer. He asked him to pick up the key.

He called the navy and talked to the detectives about the plan.

Then he told the Woodlanders, "Look, if we are guessing right, Antel and Kurt might do ANYTHING to get that clock.

"It would be far too dangerous for you to be there with us at the shop tonight.

"Two navy officers will set up a hidden video camera inside. They will film everything that happens.

"But you have to stay here where it's safe.

"I promise you, you'll see the film first thing tomorrow. And I will call as soon as there's news."

Sammy said, "Rotten rats! We will be missing out on all the good stuff!"

Mrs. Tandy said, "Well, why don't we make a double batch of oatmeal cookies while we wait?"

Chief Hemster said, "OK. Officer

Sanchez and I are leaving now. Give us fifteen minutes.

"Then, somehow, get the word out the window to those men that the clock is at the Green Forest clock shop.

"I know you'll think of some way to do it. I'm counting on you."

In fifteen minutes, Mrs. Tandy pulled open the living-room curtains.

Then she opened the two big front windows.

She called loudly, "MY, IT'S HOT IN HERE, BAKING THOSE COOKIES!"

Then Sammy walked over to a chair near the window and sat down.

He fanned himself with a dish towel and said in a loud voice, "WOW! I'M DRIPPING, I'M SO HOT!"

Bill sat down next to him.

Sammy said, "DON'T FORGET TO RE-MIND ME, BILL. FIRST THING MONDAY

I HAVE TO GO TO THE GREEN FOREST CLOCK SHOP!"

Bill said, "THEY WILL HAVE YOUR TRAVEL CLOCK FIXED BY THEN?"

Sammy shouted, "YES! YOU KNOW, IT'S JUST EXACTLY LIKE MRS. TANDY'S! I WAS SO LUCKY TO GET IT AT THE GARAGE SALE!"

Bill said, not quite so loudly, "I'll go up to get your clock with you Monday. The clock shop isn't all that far.

"Anyway, I have to go to Green Forest for some new socks."

Then Sammy got up from his chair. He said, "I GUESS IT'S COOLED OFF IN HERE NOW. HELP ME CLOSE THE WINDOWS."

When the windows and curtains were closed, the boys began to giggle.

Bill said, "I'm almost SURE I heard a noise outside. I just know they heard us."

Sammy said, "But I hate staying here and waiting. Nothing ever happens around this house."

Bill said, "Right. Nothing. Just break-ins and spies and a new baby in our basement."

Mrs. Tandy called, "Here, the cookies are almost done! Now THAT'S exciting!"

So they ate some cookies.

Then Mrs. Tandy said, "Well, let's all get into bed. It may be hours before Chief Hemster calls."

So they went to their rooms.

Hours went by.

They were sound asleep.

Suddenly, BANG! BUMP! BANG! CRASH!

The sounds came from Sammy's room.

Then there was a scream and a lot more bangs, and a thump.

Mop came bouncing and barking down the hall.

Kathy jumped out of her bed. She raced to Sammy's room.

Selma ran up the basement stairs, carrying Paul.

Bill came charging down from his end of the house.

Mrs. Tandy cut across the hall. She was holding a heavy cane in the air.

Dave called the police. Then he zoomed down the hall in his wheelchair.

Bill turned on the lights. From the

door they looked at Sammy's bed.

It was empty.

But something was bumping around on the floor between the bed and the wall!

Chapter 13: Catching the Spies

They ran around the bed.

They saw Sammy grinning up at them.

He was sitting on the stomach of a

man who lay flat on his back.

Sammy's knees were planted on each side of the man's body.

He was holding a heavy toy fire truck over his head, ready to hit the man with it.

He held his flashlight in the other hand.

"I caught Antel," he said happily. "He was sneaking in through my window.

"But he stepped right onto the pile of cars and trucks I took out for Paul to play with today.

"Look! I even got his gun!"

Sammy pointed to it lying on the floor near the door.

By that time, Selma stood in the doorway. She held Paul in her arms.

She cried, "Antel! Why are YOU here!"

He shouted, "Shut up, Selma! I came

to warn you.

"Keep quiet if you know what's good for you and your brat. Don't tell anyone anything!"

Bill said, "No, Antel, YOU keep quiet while we tie you up."

Mrs. Tandy took the cord out of her robe, and tied his hands.

Bill fished some rope out of Sammy's closet to tie Antel's feet.

By then a police car had come, with two officers. They took Antel away.

Mrs. Tandy took a good look at Selma. Her skin was pale and damp. She looked like she might faint.

Mrs. Tandy turned to the others.

She said, "Listen, let's get Selma back to bed. Then it's back to bed for us until Chief Hemster—"

She got no further.

A knock on the door announced a

smiling Chief Hemster. Next to him stood two navy officers in uniform, smiling just as widely.

Chief Hemster said, "Hi, there!"

Then he turned to the officers.

He said, "This is the family I've been telling you about! Becky Tandy. Dave Briggs. Bill Westburg. Kathy Westburg. And Sammy Westburg.

"And these two are Kurt's wife and son ... Selma Jaro and little Paul."

Sammy said, "Hey, you should have been here, Chief. You really missed out!

"Antel tried to get Selma. But WE got HIM. And now he's going to jail."

Then Sammy giggled. "I'm sure glad you made us stay here, where we'd be safe! Did you have any luck?"

Chief Hemster said, "LUCK! We caught Kurt Jaro with the goods!

"The hidden video camera worked perfectly. It filmed the break-in and Kurt's search for the clock.

"We have him opening the clock. We have him pulling the lining out of the case.

"But best of all, we have him picking a tiny strip of plastic out of the clock case, and putting it into his wallet."

Sammy said, "WHAT? That's the best

thing of all? A crummy piece of plastic?

"What about the code?

"What about the secret message?

"What about catching him red-handed? With the goods?

"A crummy piece of PLASTIC?"

Sammy looked like an angry rain cloud.

His lower lip stuck out in a pout.

But Bill was smiling, so Sammy socked him on the arm.

Bill said, "Cut it out, Sammy. They HAVE found the code. I bet that plastic was MICRO-FILM!"

One of the navy officers said, "Right, young man! Kurt Jaro was in with the submarine spies. But now we've got him.

"And you caught the man he was handing secrets to, this Antel.

"We have all we need to keep them, and Jaro's brother, in jail for life!"

Sammy said, "What a jerk! I can't believe he was willing to steal navy secrets just for money!

"And his brother was dumb enough to help do it!"

Kathy said quietly, "Selma, did you have any idea of what your husband was doing?"

Selma said, "No. He never spoke about these things in front of me. But Kurt thought I did know something.

"And he told me he would do something ... terrible ... if I called the police on him."

Dave said, "What could be more terrible than hitting you and Paul?"

Selma said, "You see, I come from Antel's country. My grandmother still lives there.

"Kurt said he would have her killed if I ever reported him to the police."

One of the navy officers said, "Mrs. Jaro, I have some sad news for you.

"In our search for information about your husband, we found out about your family, too.

"I'm sorry to tell you this, but your grandmother died three months ago.

"Your husband must have been

stealing your mail, to keep you from finding out.

"Now there's no one left that you have to protect."

Selma's eyes filled with tears. She said sadly, "Are you sure? My grandmother? She's dead?"

For a minute she sat hugging her son tightly.

Little Paul started to cry, too.

Then Selma looked up. She said, "But now my husband has no hold over me and little Paul.

"I can raise my son without being afraid anymore. My grandmother would be so glad of that."

Bill said, "This night calls for something special. I'm getting some ice cream from the freezer."

Mrs. Tandy said, "And I'll bring in the cookies, and make tea."

Kathy said, "I'll get out the milk."

Sammy said, "And I'll be looking through this Bluff Lake newspaper."

Mrs. Tandy asked, "What on earth for, Sammy?"

Sammy said, "Because I loved today so much, I'm going to see if I can find another garage sale ... for tomorrow!"